PAUL REVERE

George Sullivan

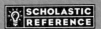

ACKNOWLEDGMENTS

Many people helped me in providing background information and illustrations to be used in this book. I'm very grateful to each of them. Special thanks are due: Patrick M. Leehey, Research Director, the Paul Revere House; Karen Otis, Museum of Fine Arts, Boston; Sal Alberti and James Lowe, James Lowe Autographs; Jenna Loosemore, American Antiquarian Society; Maja Keech, Division of Prints and Photographs, Library of Congress; Theresa Davitt, Worcester Historical Museum; Carl C. Hoss, Operations Manager, the Old North Church; Chris Steele, Massachusetts Historical Society; and Douglas Southard, the Bostonian Society.

GEORGE SULLIVAN
NEW YORK CITY

Sullivan, George, 1927–

Paul Revere/George Sullivan

p.   cm.—(In their own words)

Includes bibliographical references.

Summary: A biography of the man made famous by a poem about the American Revolution, placing his life and work in real historical context.

LIBRARY OF CONGRESS CATALOGING-IN-PUBLICATION DATA

1. Revere, Paul, 1735–1818 Juvenile literature. 2. Statesman—Massachusetts Biography Juvenile literature. 3. Massachusetts Biography Juvenile literature. 4. Massachusetts—History—Revolution, 1775–1783 Juvenile literature. [1. Revere, Paul, 1735–1818.   2. United States—History—Revolution. 1775–1783 Biography.   3. Silversmiths.] I. Title. II. Series: In their own words (Scholastic)   F69.R43S85   1999   973.3'311'092—dc21 99-17381 [B]   CIP

ISBN 0-439-14748-4 (pob)
ISBN 0-439-09552-2 (pb)
10 9 8 7 6 5 4 3 2 1   0/0   01   02   03   04

Composition by Brad Walrod

Printed in the U.S.A.   23

First trade printing, September 2000

CHAPTER 1

INTRODUCTION

"HAVING A LITTLE LEISURE, I WISH to fulfill my promise of giving you some facts... which I do not remember to have seen in any history of the American Revolution."

With these words, Paul Revere began a letter to Jeremy Belknap of the Massachusetts Historical Society. In it, Revere told the story of his midnight ride on the night of April 18, 1775.

The letter was eight pages long. It gave new facts about the famous ride. Belknap put the date of January 1, 1798, on the letter.

Since then, much has been written about Paul Revere and his famous ride. Some of it is false. Some of it is folklore.

That's why serious students refer to Paul Revere's own account of the ride. It is a plain and factual account of what took place. (It also shows that Paul Revere was not always a good speller. Get was always git. Alarm had two l's.)

Artists' drawings of the midnight ride almost always picture Paul Revere as a lone rider.

In trying to answer questions about the past, historians use different kinds of sources. There are primary sources and secondary sources. Primary sources are actual records that have been handed down from the past.

Letters, diaries, speeches, and official records are primary sources. Paul Revere's letter describing his midnight ride is a primary source. So is the Declaration of Independence. So is your birth certificate.

Secondary sources are descriptions of an event written by someone who did not witness it. A history textbook is a secondary source. The *World Book* and *Collier's* encyclopedias are secondary sources.

Besides his account of his ride, there are many other primary sources that relate to Paul Revere. He was well known as an artist. Original copies of more than two dozen of his drawings are owned by the American Antiquarian Society. Some of these drawings offer clues to Paul Revere's character.

Paul Revere was a skilled silversmith. Silver bowls,

spoons, teapots, and other objects that he made are in the public collections of several museums. These include the Museum of Fine Arts in Boston, the Metropolitan Museum of Art in New York, and the Worcester (Massachusetts) Art Museum.

The city of Boston offers other primary sources. There's the Revere House itself and the Old North Church. There's also the Old Granary Burying Ground, where Paul Revere is buried. In Boston's North End, you can walk the narrow streets where Paul Revere once lived and worked.

This biography of Paul Revere includes both primary and secondary sources. Quoted material comes from Paul Revere's own accounts of his ride. It comes from letters that he wrote and his business records.

To illustrate this book, copies of Revere's drawings have been used. These have been combined with drawings by other artists, copies of paintings, and modern photographs.

People who lived many years ago left many clues about their lives. They wrote letters. They kept diaries. They recorded their family trees. They kept business records. They took photographs.

Many sources of information about the past have been lost or destroyed. But some primary sources still exist. They give us a tiny view of what the past was really like.

BOSTON BOYHOOD

PAUL REVERE, AMERICAN PATRIOT, was born in Boston in December 1734. The precise date is not known.

Paul Revere's parents had eleven or twelve children. Only seven lived to be adults. Paul was the oldest boy.

It was exciting to grow up in Boston. As the main seaport of the American colonies, Boston was a noisy, busy place.

Boston had a population of 15,000 people, large for the time. These citizens were crowded into a town that was almost completely surrounded by water. It was joined to the rest of the Massachusetts Bay Colony by a narrow strip of land. This narrow strip of land is called a neck.

At high tide, the sea sometimes flooded over the neck. Then Boston became an island.

No part of Boston was far from the wharves where sailing ships were docked. They were always being loaded or unloaded. Barrels, filled with molasses for making rum, were stacked on the wharves. From England came tea, ribbons and fabric, paper, glass, and ironware.

Most Bostonians lived in wood-frame or brick houses. They were usually two or three stories high. But Boston was also a city of large homes. These were owned by wealthy doctors, lawyers, and merchants. Churches dotted the landscape. Many of these houses and churches still stand.

The town's narrow, crooked streets were busy with horse carts and freight wagons. When crossing streets, a child had to watch out for horses' hooves and heavy wagon wheels.

Boston was a city of sailors, sail makers, tailors, wig makers, soap boilers, rope makers, and silversmiths.

Fish peddlers with their tin horns announced the

A view of Boston from the 1700s. Later, when married and living at North Square, Paul Revere had his silversmith's shop on Clark's Wharf in Boston Harbor.

arrival of fresh cod, mackerel, and haddock. "Lob, lob, lob," shouted lobstermen, who pushed their colorful carts. Oystermen, with their stock in sacks on their backs, added to the noise.

Chimney sweeps also sold their services. They

carried brooms to sweep the soot and blankets to carry it away.

Boston was a city of bells. Church bells were used to call Bostonians to church or meetings. They rang in honor of holidays or anniversaries. They rang to signal the opening of markets. Bells rang to honor the dead. They rang for fires. Schoolteachers rang bells for school.

Puritans had founded Boston more than a century before, in 1630. The Puritans were a group of Protestants who wanted simpler forms of religious worship and stricter rules of behavior. They were treated badly in England for their beliefs.

Paul's father, Apollos Rivoire, came to America from France at the age of thirteen.

Apollos left his homeland because of his beliefs. The Rivoires were Protestant. France was mainly a Catholic country at the time. The French Catholics often abused Protestants who lived there.

When Apollos traveled to America, his uncle paid for the trip. His uncle also arranged for Apollos to become an apprentice to a silversmith.

As an apprentice, Apollos worked learning his trade. He was not paid. He received food, a place to sleep, and clothing. After seven years, he could become a master workman with a shop of his own.

In time, it became obvious that Apollos was a highly talented craftsperson. Most of the time he created silver pieces. He also made small gold items, such as rings and buttons.

Sometime during the 1720s, Apollos Rivoire opened his own silversmithing shop. He changed his name to Paul Revere. Since most Bostonians spoke English, he thought this name would be easier to pronounce.

Paul Revere, Sr., married Deborah Hitchborn in 1729. The Reveres had no children for almost three years. Then a girl, named Deborah after her mother, was born. Three years later, Paul arrived. After Paul, the Reveres had five more children.

The Revere family lived in a house on Fish Street. It was near the wharves where the ships docked. It was a good place for a silversmith to live. Many of Mr. Revere's customers were ships' captains or worked in nearby shops.

Paul and his brothers and sisters probably slept in the attic of their Fish Street home. Their playmates were their Hitchborn cousins.

Some families sent their young children to "infant schools." These cost a penny a week. There they learned their ABCs and some reading. They also learned to say "please" and "thank you" and other rules of politeness.

When Paul was about seven, he started attending Boston's North Writing School. It was in a two-story building. Students, sitting on rough benches, were taught writing on one floor and reading on the other. Only boys attended the school.

Paul stopped going to school when he was thirteen. Many boys became apprentices at this age. So it was with Paul. He went to work with his father to learn to be a silversmith.

Near Paul's house was a tall church called Christ Church. It later became the Old North Church. It was also called Eight Bell Church because of its set of eight English bells. Their tone was so clear that the bells could be heard across the Charles River in Cambridge.

Paul Revere learned the trade of silversmithing from his father and was deeply influenced by him—as these two containers for spices, called casters, indicate. Paul Revere made the one on the left; his father made the one on the right.

As young teenagers, Paul and his friends were fascinated by the bells. They formed a bell-ringers' club.

The boys set down rules for their club in a formal document. They decided that "...none shall be admitted as a member of this Society without unanimous Vote of Members then Present...."

The boys agreed "To Ring any Time when the Wardens of the Church . . . shall desire it. . . ." If they did not answer the warden's call, they were fined three shillings.

Paul and six of his friends signed the document. Paul's signature is easy to pick out. It includes decorative strokes of the pen beneath his name. He signed his name this way for the rest of his life.

The bell-ringers' agreement shows that Paul and his friends understood the importance of serving their community. It also shows that they knew about self-government and the rule of the majority. Boston patriots would later struggle to win these rights.

Paul's father died during the summer of 1754. Paul was nineteen. He was, by law, too young to take over his father's silversmithing business. Ownership passed to his mother. But it was Paul who carried on the work.

Paul was supporting his mother and his six brothers and sisters. His oldest sister, Deborah, was getting ready to marry and leave the Revere family.

We the Subscribers Do agree To the following
Articles Viz

That if we Can have Liberty From the wardens
of Doctors Cutllers church we will attend there once
a week on Evenings To Ring the Bells for two hours
Each Time from the date here of for one year

That we will Choose a Moderator Every three Month
whose Busfiness fhall be To give out the Changes
and other Busfiness as fhall be Agreed by a Majority
of Voices then Prefent

That None shall Be admitted a Member of this Society
without a Unanimous Vote of the Members then Prefent
and that No member Shall begg Money of any Person
In the Tower on Penalty of being Excluded the Society
and that we will Attend To Ring at any Time when the Wardn.
of the Church Aforesaid shall desire it on Penalty of Paying
three fhillings for the good of the Society Provided we Can
have the whole Care of the Bells

That the Members of this Society fhall nott Exceed
Eight Persons

and all Differences To be deided By a Majority of Voices

                                        John Dyer
                                        Paul Revere,
                                        Iliah Flagg
                                        Barth Ballard
                                        Jonathan Law
                                        Jon.ᵃ Brown jun.ʳ
                                        Joseph Snelling

Bell-ringers' agreement signed by seven boys of Boston, including Paul Revere, who was about fifteen at the time.

His brother Thomas helped Paul in the silversmith's shop. Thomas later was to become a silversmith himself. John, his youngest brother, was to become an apprentice tailor.

In the spring of 1756, Paul was twenty-one. He suddenly gave up silversmithing and supporting the family. A war was the reason.

Long before Paul was born, a few countries of Europe fought several wars. These wars were fought to decide which country would control North America. Each country wanted both the land and natural riches the continent offered. Colonial America was also looked upon as a large new market for their goods.

These wars had many names. There was King William's War, Queen Anne's War, and King George's War. The name Paul knew best was the Seven Years War. Later there was the French and Indian War.

After years of war, two nations remained in the struggle, England and France. The French controlled Canada and the land known as Louisiana.

But the French wanted more. They wanted land that the British believed to be theirs. French troops, along with their Native American allies, came down from Canada to raid British settlements in New York and Massachusetts.

In 1756, England and France went to war. The governor of Massachusetts called for about 3,500 volunteers to help the English fight the French.

Paul was one of those who answered the call. Maybe he felt it was his duty as a citizen. Maybe he looked upon military service as a great adventure. Or maybe it was just a chance to do something different.

Whatever the reason, Paul set aside his silversmith's hammer and apron and his role as supporter of the Revere family. In exchange, Paul, as a second lieutenant, was given a blanket, a bowl, and two spoons. He was also given a uniform that included a blue coat and red pants. In his belt, he carried a hatchet.

Paul, like other volunteers, brought along his own rifle. The colony provided gunpowder and a powder

George Washington, in his early twenties at the time, played an active role in the French and Indian War, leading a military force against the French. His experience helped Washington later become Commander of the Continental army.

horn in which to store it. The colony also gave him bullets, a bullet pouch, and a knapsack. Paul was paid about $3 a month.

In the spring of 1756, Paul and his fellow volunteers were sent to Albany, New York. The long line of men, with their supply wagons and cannons drawn by horses and oxen, moved slowly west across Massachusetts into New York. At Albany, they joined troops from other colonies. Then they marched north to Fort William Henry on Lake George in New York. There they camped.

The camp was smelly and dirty. Many of the men got sick.

Paul saw no Native Americans or French that summer. There were, however, rumors of Native American raiding parties.

Boredom was Paul's chief enemy. He spent much of his time cleaning his rifle and scratching black-fly bites.

Near the end of November, the Massachusetts troops were ordered home.

When Paul finally reached the town gate and entered Boston, he must have felt a great sense of relief. His military service was over. It was good to be back home.

COLONIAL
SILVERSMITH

PAUL REVERE RETURNED TO BOSTON
following his service as an army volunteer.
There he met twenty-year-old Sara Orne.
On August 17, 1757, Paul and Sara were married.

Little is known of Sara. In the family Bible,
where family records are set down, Paul wrote her
name as "Sary." It is likely he called her by that
name.

Paul and his bride went to live at his mother's.
His brothers, Thomas and John, and his sisters,
Frances, Betty, and Mary, also lived in the house.
In the homes of colonial America, privacy was
rare.

The following spring Sara gave birth to their

first child. She was named Deborah. Sara was to give birth seven more times. Three of her eight children died as infants.

Paul Revere went to work every day as a silversmith. Paul was lucky. The silversmith's shop he had inherited from his father was fully equipped. In fact, Paul used molds his father had used in casting silver pieces.

Paul's shop produced a great variety of silver items. Many were for drinking. These included cups and tall mugs with handles and hinged covers. These were called tankards.

He produced an endless stream of buckles, buttons, and rings.

He made spoons—teaspoons, tablespoons, and salt spoons. He made silver trays and serving dishes. He made shakers, called casters, for spices.

He made toy whistles for children. He once made a silver collar for a man's pet squirrel.

Like any silversmith, Paul did a good deal of repair work. He mended the lids of tankards. He "took out bruises" from worn pieces. He cleaned and restored the silvery shine to casters and other items.

Bostonians loved drinking tea, a practice brought from England. For preparing tea and drinking it, Paul's shop made teapots, cream pots, and sugar dishes. The shop also turned out sugar tongs (for serving small pieces of sugar).

Paul Revere made this sturdy silver tankard in 1768.

Paul worked in gold, too. But the gold pieces were usually smaller objects—buttons, beads, and rings.

Many of Paul's pieces were made for rich families of the day. These he decorated with the family's initials or crest.

As Paul's business grew, he hired other silversmiths to help out. These were men who had finished their apprenticeships. But they lacked the money to go into business for themselves.

During his years as a silversmith, Paul kept careful record books. He wrote the name of each customer in his books. He listed what type of object he made for each of them. He put down the amount each paid, and how they paid. Some gave him "hard money." Others traded rum, fish, or old silver pieces.

Paul listed how much money his brother Thomas owed him. Paul charged Thomas for his meals and rent for his room in the Revere house. Paul lent Thomas the money to buy knee buckles, a silk handkerchief, yarn stockings, and a secondhand wig. Men of fashion wore wigs during these times.

Museums and historical societies now own many of Paul Revere's silver pieces. This sauceboat, which Revere made in 1765, is on exhibit at New York's Metropolitan Museum of Art.

Paul also charged rent and lent money to his youngest brother, John. John had become a tailor.

Paul used the skills he had learned as a silversmith to develop other businesses. He cut detailed designs into small, thin, flat sheets of copper. Called engravings, these copperplates were then used by Boston printers to illustrate books, newspapers, and handbills.

Paul also learned to make false teeth. In colonial times, when a person had a bad toothache, the tooth was pulled. Dentists did not fill teeth.

There was a great need for false teeth as a result. Paul carved his false teeth from hippopotamus tusks.

The extra money that Paul earned helped to pay the rent and other bills. The Revere family, while not rich, lived well.

His work took most of his time. But Paul Revere was always very loving to his children. He called them "his lambs."

Beginning in 1763, Boston was hit by an outbreak of smallpox. Smallpox begins with a fever. Then red spots break out, usually on the face. As the fever rises, the red spots form blisters. These often leave scars—"pocks"—on the face.

One of Paul's small children got smallpox. Because the disease spreads easily from one person to the next, Paul was ordered to bring the child to a local pesthouse. These were houses that were set aside for people with easily spread diseases.

Paul refused to bring the child to the pesthouse.

In February 1770, Paul Revere bought this home on North Square in Boston. It had been built around 1680. (In Revere's time, another house was located to the left, right alongside the Revere house.) The Reveres lived in the house for about ten years.

He knew that a stay in a pesthouse usually resulted in death.

Paul and Sara cared for the child at home. The town then ordered that no one could enter or leave Paul's house. The house was made to fly a smallpox flag. A guard was put outside the house to keep Paul and his family inside.

Week after week, the Reveres remained locked up inside their own home. Paul's record books show that there were no orders for silver during this time.

Months later, the child recovered from the disease. But she remained sickly. The child died before her first birthday.

One of Paul's customers was John Singleton Copley, a noted portrait painter. Paul made silver frames for small paintings done by Copley.

Around 1770, Copley agreed to paint Paul's portrait. Paul was about thirty-five years old.

Copley painted Paul at his worktable in his silversmith's shop He has an unfinished teapot in one hand. In front of him are the tools of a silversmith.

John Singleton Copley's portrait of his friend Paul Revere. The picture was painted when Paul was in his mid-thirties.

Paul wears a handsome shirt made of fine linen and a vest with solid gold buttons. He rests his chin on one hand. He seems to be thinking about what to engrave on the side of the teapot.

BLOODSHED

GREAT BRITAIN'S LONG WAR WITH France finally ended in 1763. The English had won. Britain got almost all the French land in Canada plus other French colonies in North America.

But peace also brought problems for the British. The war was very costly. Keeping military forces in North America was another big expense. The British needed to get money from the American colonies in the form of taxes.

In 1764, the British Parliament passed the Sugar Act. It placed a tax of three pennies on each gallon of molasses being sent to the colonies.

The Sugar Act was hard on the colonists. The

Quartering Act and the Stamp Act, passed in 1765, were worse. The Quartering Act ordered colonists to provide British soldiers with places to live. The colonists also were made to supply the soldiers with food, candles, cider, or beer.

The Stamp Act required colonists to pay for tax stamps. These stamps were required on newspapers, marriage licenses, playing cards, and some legal documents.

Colonists such as Paul Revere looked upon the Stamp Act in horror. They were used to making their own rules. They didn't like the idea of having to obey laws they did not help to create. They didn't like what they called "taxation without representation."

Paul Revere had always been a great joiner. He had joined a military unit to fight the French in the French and Indian War. He had joined the Masons, a secret society meant to promote brotherly love. He would be a lifelong member of the Masons.

Now Paul began joining groups that would resist the Stamp Act. One was the Long Room Club. Started in 1762, the Long Room Club was one of the first secret clubs that helped to hatch the American Revolution.

Paul would spend long hours in his shop each day. At the end of the day, he locked up his shop. Then Paul often headed for the private back room of a tavern and a meeting of the Long Room Club.

Samuel Adams was one of the leaders of the Long Room Club. Adams was a member of the Massachusetts legislature. The legislature was the colony's chief lawmaking body. Adams, who was twelve years older than Paul Revere, was to become a powerful and tireless force in the Revolutionary movement.

John Hancock, one of Boston's richest merchants, was another member of the Long Room Club. Hancock used his money and power to help the cause of independence. The British would soon come to see him as one of the most dangerous of all Revolutionary leaders.

In the summer of 1765, Paul joined another patriotic society called the Sons of Liberty. Members fought hard against the Stamp Act. They were

Samuel Adams did much to stir opposition to British rule. He was a second cousin of John Adams, who would become the second American president.

active not just in Massachusetts but all the way from South Carolina to New Hampshire.

Riots broke out in protest of the Stamp Act. Angry colonists refused to permit the tax stamps to be sold.

Paul used his skill in engraving copperplates to

support the spirit of resistance. In one cartoonlike engraving, Paul paid tribute to the "Boston brave" for protecting Lady Liberty against the hateful British dragon.

In 1766, the British ended the Stamp Act. The next year, however, the British Parliament passed the Townshend Acts.

The Townshend Acts called for a duty to be collected on such imported goods as glass, paint, lead, and tea. The colonists said the duties were the same as taxes. To protest, they stopped buying goods from England.

In Massachusetts, the legislature sent a letter to each of the other colonies. The letter asked colonists to take a stand against the taxes.

British leaders boiled with rage. King George III himself spoke out. He ordered the Massachusetts legislature to take back the letter.

The legislature turned its back on the king. By a vote of 92 to 17, the legislature refused to obey the king's order.

This was a great victory for the Sons of Liberty.

They wanted to keep alive the memory of the day.
So, they asked Paul to make a silver punch bowl.
The bowl would list the names of the ninety-two
members of the legislature who refused to obey the
king.

The handsome silver bowl that Paul created is
now looked upon as a national treasure. It is
considered to be almost as important as the
Declaration of Independence. Besides the names,
Paul engraved the sides of the bowl with several

*In 1768, Paul Revere was asked to make this silver punch bowl. It
honors the ninety-two members of the Massachusetts legislature who
refused to obey King George's order to take back their letter of protest
against the Townshend Acts.*

symbols of liberty. One of these was the Magna Carta, the British bill of rights.

Creating the silver bowl wasn't all that Paul did to protest the Townshend Acts. He and several other members of the Sons of Liberty would go out on moonless nights. They would paint their faces black and pull white nightcaps down over their heads. They would make a quick appearance at the home of a person whose job it was to collect the taxes. Windows might be broken and threats made. Little wonder that some of the frightened tax collectors left Boston.

The British government thought of the colonists as children who were being bad. To make them behave, the British sent a fleet of warships to Boston. The ships sailed into Boston Harbor on the last day of September in 1768. They were loaded with British professional soldiers, called regulars.

Paul described the scene that day and the next:

On Friday, Sept 30, 1768, the ships of war arrived schooners transports etc. came up the harbour and anchored around the Town; their cannons loaded, a spring on their cables, as for a regular seige. At noon on Saturday the fourteenth and twenty-nineth regements and a detachment from the 59th regement, and a train of artillery landed on Long Wharf; there formed and marched with insolent parade, drums beating, fifes playing, up King Street each [soldier] having received sixteen rounds of powder and ball.

The arrival of the soldiers in Boston made things worse. There were angry words between the soldiers and local citizens. Young boys sometimes made fun of the soldiers. They called them "bloody backs" or "lobsters" because of the red jackets they wore.

Boston was like a ticking time bomb. On Monday, March 5, 1770, the bomb exploded.

It was a cold, gray day. The ground was snow-covered. That morning there had been a fight between a group of soldiers and a local worker. Both sides were in an ugly mood.

Later in the day, a boy who had been teasing a

British guard was knocked to the ground. An angry crowd gathered.

The guard lost his temper. He demanded that the boy come forward and "show his face." More people joined the group. The guard hit the boy.

The crowd was furious. Terrified, the guard called for help. Captain Thomas Preston, a British officer, and several regulars came to the guard's aid.

The crowd, now an angry mob of hundreds, pressed toward the soldiers, swinging sticks and their fists. Then came the words, "Present . . ." and "Fire!"

Shots rang out. Five men died. These were the first colonists to give up their lives in protesting British policies.

Captain Preston prevented his soldiers from firing a second time. The crowd broke up. Most people hurried to their homes.

Before the next day, Captain Preston and eight of his men were under arrest for murder. Preston was tried and cleared of any guilt. But two of his soldiers were found guilty of manslaughter. As punishment, they were branded on their thumbs.

Historians are not sure where Paul Revere was that night. Some believe that Paul was there because he made a pen-and-ink drawing of the site.

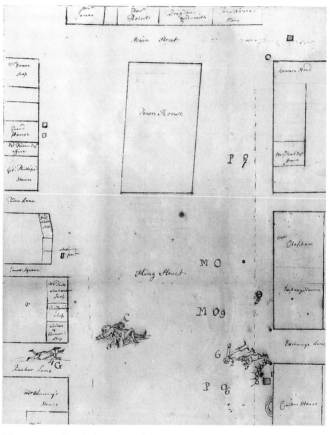

This pen-and-ink drawing of the Boston Massacre by Paul Revere was used in court during the trial of Captain Preston and his soldiers.

It shows where the soldiers stood and the victims fell.

The incident quickly came to be known as the Boston Massacre, and even the Bloody Boston Massacre. A massacre, says the dictionary, is the murder of a large number of people. The break in the peace that winter night in Boston, while tragic, was not a massacre. But some patriot speech makers used the word to whip up anti-British feelings.

Paul Revere used his talents to help the cause. After the violence, he made an engraving of a drawing by an artist named Henry Pelham. It was said to picture the shooting at the moment it took place. It shows a line of evil-faced British soldiers firing into a crowd of peaceful citizens. Widely printed and copied, the engraving helped to arouse the anger of colonists.

The Boston Massacre wasn't the only outbreak of violence. Earlier in 1770, a frightened British tax collector fired into a mob that had gathered in front of his house. A young boy named Christopher Seider was killed.

The patriots wanted to remember the boy who had died for their cause. Special ceremonies were planned on the first anniversary of his death.

Paul held a silent evening ceremony in honor of young Christopher. It also was meant to honor the victims of the Boston Massacre. Every window of

Paul Revere's version of "The Bloody Massacre" is probably the best known of his engravings. It depicts British soldiers, at the command of their leader, firing at peaceful, defenseless citizens.

Paul's North Square home was lighted with a special scene.

In one window was the ghostly figure of the murdered boy. In another, there was a picture to represent the Boston Massacre. In still another was the figure of an American woman wearing a liberty cap on her head.

Outside the house, a huge crowd gathered in silent tribute.

In reporting on the event, the *Boston Gazette* declared:

In the evening, there was a very striking exhibition at the dwelling house of Mr. Paul Revere, fronting old North Square . . . the spectators, which amounted to many thousands, were struck with solemn silence and their faces covered with melancholy gloom.

CHAPTER 5

TEA PARTY

IN THE MONTHS THAT FOLLOWED THE Boston Massacre, Paul Revere worked at his silversmith's shop during the day. He also continued as an active member of the Masons, the Sons of Liberty, and other groups.

Paul's duties as a Mason were especially important to him. Late in 1770, he was elected Master of the St. Andrew's [Masonic] Lodge. His duties were to conduct meetings and "maintain the honor and dignity of the Lodge."

At the same time, Paul continued to attend secret political meetings.

On May 23, 1773, something terrible happened in Paul Revere's life. Sara Orne Revere, his thirty-seven-year-old wife, died. Her death came five months after she gave birth to their eighth child, Isanna. Paul buried Sara in Boston's Old Granary Burying Ground.

Before the year ended, Paul married a second time. It was common for both widows and widowers to remarry soon after the death of their spouses.

A miniature portrait of Rachel Revere, painted when she was about thirty-nine.

This time his bride was Rachel Walker. Rachel was a lively young woman. Paul called her his "Dear Girl."

Paul Revere wrote poetry for his new wife. He wrote one poem on the back of a bill for mending a spoon. The lines of the poem spelled out Rachel's name:

> *Take three fourths of a Paine that makes*
> *Traitors confess [Rac(k)]*
> *With three parts of a place which the*
> *Wicked don't bless [Hel(l)]*

Joyne four sevenths of an Exercise which
*   shop-keepers use [Walk(ing)]*
And what Bad men do, when they good
*   actions refuse [Er(r)]*
These four added together with great
*   care and Art*
Will point out the Fair One nearest
*   my Heart.*

Eight children were born to Rachel and Paul. Three of the babies died young. The children who survived were Joshua, Joseph, Harriet, Maria, and John.

At the same time that Paul was marrying Rachel Walker, the colonists faced a new problem. Tea was the trouble this time.

The British had ended the Townshend Acts. But they had left a tax on tea. It was very small. The British believed the colonists would not mind paying it. But the colonists did mind. They knew that if they paid, the British Parliament would think it had the right to tax the colonies.

The colonists found out that ships loaded with tea were being sent from England. They were furious.

The first ship to arrive in Boston was the *Dartmouth*. Almost from the minute that it docked at Griffin's Wharf, armed colonists watched the vessel. The Sons of Liberty asked these men to make sure that none of the tea was unloaded. Paul is likely to have been one of those who stayed up all night guarding the ship.

There was no sleep for Paul the next day. Sam Adams and other patriot leaders wanted to get a message to patriots in nearby cities. They wanted to warn them that British tea ships might be coming. There was no telegraph or telephone in those days. There was not even regular postal service. If you wanted to send a letter or a message, you hired a messenger.

The patriot leaders chose six colonists to carry their warning message. One of the six was Paul Revere. On the last day of November 1773, Paul made his first ride for the patriot cause.

Before long, two more tea ships, the *Eleanor* and the *Beaver*, arrived in Boston. They carried more than 300 chests of tea valued at around $90,000. The ships were guarded day and night to make sure that no tea was taken off the vessels.

Angry citizens gathered at the Old South Church. They decided that the tea ships must return to England. But there was a problem. Under the law, no ship could leave the port of Boston unless it had unloaded all of its cargo.

The law also stated that a ship must be unloaded within twenty days. Otherwise, the ship's cargo could be seized and sold at auction. The colonists did not want this to happen to tea from England. If it did happen, taxes would still have to be paid.

December 16 marked the nineteenth day that the *Dartmouth* had been in port. The ship's captain begged the governor of Massachusetts to let him sail.

The governor refused. The deadline kept getting closer. Tension was at the bursting point.

The Sons of Liberty were prepared for the

governor's refusal. At the Old South Church, when the announcement came, there were cheers and shouts of joy. "To Griffin's Wharf!" someone shouted. "Boston Harbor a teapot tonight!" someone else cried out.

The mob poured out onto the street. Boys and men hurried to their homes to disguise themselves as Native Americans. They smeared their faces with grease and soot and added streaks of red paint.

They also pulled stocking caps over their heads. Some stuck feathers in their hair and draped blankets over their shoulders. Then each of these "Indians" grabbed an ax and headed for Griffin's Wharf to join the other Sons of Liberty.

There was no shouting. No one was unruly. The group of about 150 men and boys approached the pier quietly. They hardly even spoke. At the wharf, they divided into three groups. Each of the three groups was assigned to one of the tea-carrying ships.

Once aboard, they asked for the keys to the holds where the tea was stored. The men then hauled the

At Griffin's Wharf in Boston on the night of December 16, 1773, Bostonians disguised as Native Americans staged the Boston Tea Party.

big tea chests up onto the deck. They broke them open with their axes and dumped the tea into the harbor.

A large crowd watched as the men worked. So

much tea was dumped into the harbor that it piled up in the water. Some of it sloshed back onto the decks. Men quickly shoveled the tea back into the water.

Although the men worked quickly, their task took all night. When they were finished, the Sons of Liberty went home. They washed off the grease, soot, and paint, and went to bed. The event came to be known as the Boston Tea Party.

A poem praised Paul Revere and Dr. Joseph Warren, a well-known patriot leader, for the role each had played in the tea party.

> Rally Mohawks! Bring out your axes,
> And tell King George we'll pay no taxes
>   On his foreign tea . . .
> Our Warren's there, and bold Revere
> With hands to do and words to cheer
>   For Liberty and laws

The colonists wrote a report about the tea party. It told why the event was necessary. The report had to be delivered to colonists in New York and Philadelphia. Several men offered to make the delivery. Paul was chosen.

Paul set out on the day after the Tea Party. He covered almost 350 miles before he reached Philadelphia. Fall changed to winter during Paul's journey. The days were cold and darkness came quickly. Riding conditions were poor on the rough roads. Yet Paul completed his trip and was back in Boston in eleven days. No rider had ever done anything like that before.

After the Boston Tea Party, the British decided that the citizens of Massachusetts must be made to pay for what they had done. Early in 1774, a British ship named the *Lively* arrived in Boston. It was full of soldiers, The ship also carried the news of how the colonists were to be punished.

First, the port of Boston was to be closed. No ships would be allowed to go in or out. The people of Boston had to agree to pay for the tea that had been destroyed or the port would not reopen.

Second, there was to be a new legal system.

Townspeople accused of serious crimes would now be sent to London for trial.

Third, the activities of the Massachusetts legislature were to be cut back. New powers were to be given to the governor of Massachusetts. The governor now would be like a dictator.

King George named Lieutenant General Thomas Gage as the new governor. At the time, Gage commanded all British forces in North America.

The British called the new measures Coercive Acts. They were meant to coerce the colonists, that is, to force them to do what the British wanted.

But to the colonists they were the Intolerable Acts, meaning that they were like a very bad toothache. They were too painful to be endured.

Not long after the *Lively* docked in Boston with news of the Intolerable Acts, Paul was called upon again. He was to ride to New York and Philadelphia. There he was to help organize resistance to the Acts.

In the summer of 1774, a meeting was held to discuss what could be done about the Intolerable Acts. Patriots representing various towns in Suffolk

County, Massachusetts, which included Boston, were there. At the meeting, Dr. Joseph Warren wrote the "Suffolk Resolves." Dr. Warren had written and spoken frequently for the patriot cause.

The Suffolk Resolves called upon the people of Massachusetts to form their own government. If the British tried to stop them, they were ready to fight for their cause.

After the meeting, Paul was assigned to travel to New York and Philadelphia once again. This time he carried the Suffolk Resolves. This was Paul's most important mission yet.

At Carpenters' Hall in Philadelphia, the First Continental Congress was in session. Representatives from all the colonies except Georgia were part of the Congress. Samuel Adams and John Adams were there. They represented Massachusetts. George Washington and Patrick Henry were Virginia's representatives.

Paul left Boston on September 11, 1774. Incredibly, he arrived in Philadelphia only five days later.

The day after he delivered the document, the

Paul Revere made his first ride as a messenger for the Revolutionary cause in November 1773. In September 1774, he was called upon again. This time he carried the Suffolk Resolves.

Continental Congress gave its approval to the Suffolk Resolves. An important step had been taken on the road to revolution.

Between 1773 and 1775, Paul made as many as six trips from Boston to New York and Philadelphia. Almost always he hired horses for this work. He once made the journey in a small horse-drawn carriage.

Paul made many short trips from Boston to other New England cities and towns. He was called a "messenger," a "courier," or an "express."

But Paul Revere was more than merely a rider

who carried messages. Because of his travels, he knew all of the important patriots in the northeast. Within Boston he was a member of the Sons of Liberty. He belonged to other groups that supported the Revolutionary cause. He helped each group to understand what other groups were thinking, planning, and doing. He had taken on a crucial role in the Revolutionary movement that was gathering steam throughout the colonies.

THE MIDNIGHT RIDE

ARCH 5, 1775, WAS A BIG DAY for the colonists. It was the fifth anniversary of the Boston Massacre. A mass meeting was held at the Old South Church. John Hancock and Samuel Adams were there. Paul Revere was no doubt there, too.

They listened as Dr. Joseph Warren and others spoke. They lashed out at the British for their unfair tax laws.

General Gage sent several British soldiers to the meeting. He told them to listen to the speeches. If any of the patriots went too far in their words of protest, the soldiers were to arrest them.

But there were no arrests. General Gage did not want to do anything that would make things more tense.

Meanwhile, General Gage's superiors in London were losing patience with him. They sent the general new orders. They told him to get tougher. They told him to arrest those causing the trouble.

The patriot leaders in Boston soon learned of General Gage's new orders. They were filled with fear at the thought of being arrested. Many of them fled from Boston. John Hancock and Sam Adams hurried off to the town of Lexington, about twenty-five miles north and west of Boston.

Dr. Warren stayed in Boston, despite the risk of being arrested. Paul Revere stayed, too.

From their spies, the British learned that the patriots were preparing for action. They had stored arms and gunpowder in the farm village of Concord. This news angered General Gage. He decided to send some of his troops to Concord to capture or destroy the weapons.

By April 15, a Saturday, Boston was tense.

Something was about to happen. North Square was filled with British soldiers. On the Charles River, British warships had lowered their transport boats into the water.

The next day, Sunday, April 16, Paul Revere rode to Lexington. There he met with John Hancock and Sam Adams. He told the patriot leaders what the British soldiers were doing.

Paul Revere's travels upset General Gage. He didn't like the idea that Paul was spreading news about his troops. The general knew that Paul and the other riders had to be stopped. Otherwise, he would not be able to capture the weapons stored at Concord.

General Gage ordered twenty of his men to patrol the roads between Boston and Concord. The *Somerset*, a huge British warship, was anchored in the Charles River. It had a role to play, too. It was meant to prevent Paul and other alarm riders from crossing the river. Once across, they could ride on to Lexington and Concord.

Dr. Warren learned from a secret source that the

British troops would soon be on the move. It was time for action.

Sometime between nine and ten o'clock on Tuesday night, April 18, Dr. Warren sent a message to Paul. In it, he asked Paul to come at once.

Dr. Warren told Paul that he wanted him to ride out to Lexington again. Once there, he was to warn John Hancock and Samuel Adams that the British soldiers were coming. Paul was also to alarm citizens along the way. They then could prepare to defend themselves.

It is likely that Paul was also told to continue on to Concord. There he would check that the hidden stores of weapons were safe and sound.

"Doctor Warren sent in great haste for me," Paul was later to write, "and begged that I would immediately set off for Lexington, where Messrs Hancock and Adams were, and acquaint them of the movement, and that it was thought they were the objects."

Dr. Warren knew that British soldiers were guarding the roads between Boston and Concord.

Dr. Joseph Warren was one of the most admired and respected of the Revolutionary leaders. It was Warren who called upon Paul Revere to ride to Lexington to warn Samuel Adams and John Hancock of the approach of the British regulars.

To be sure that his message got through, Dr. Warren explained to Paul that he had already sent a second messenger to Lexington.

The second messenger was William Dawes. Dawes was a Boston leather maker. He was a loyal patriot. Yet, he was not as well known to the British as Paul. For this reason, Dr. Warren believed that it might be easier for Dawes to get by the British soldiers.

Dr. Warren assigned the two riders different routes. Dawes had left Boston by traveling across Boston Neck. This was the narrow strip that linked the city to the mainland.

Paul was to set off in a different direction. Paul's route was to take him by boat across the Charles River to Charlestown. Once there, he was to be given a horse. He was then to gallop on to Lexington and Concord.

In case he was not able to cross the Charles River, Paul had already arranged a clever way of warning the people of Charlestown of British plans. He would have a signal light hung in the bell tower of the Old North Church. The church was the tallest building in Boston at the time.

Two lanterns were to be hung if the English were coming by water. One lantern would mean they were coming by land.

As Paul would later write:

I agreed with Colonel Conant and some other gentlemen, that if the British went out by water, we would [show] two lanthorns in the North Church steeple, and if by land, one, as a signal, for we were apprehensive it would be difficult to cross the Charles River, or git over Boston neck.

(At the time, *lanthorn* was a word the people of Massachusetts used for lantern.)

Paul had friends and neighbors who would help him in hanging the signal lights. Before leaving on his ride, Paul told his friends to go to the Old North Church and hang two lanterns in the steeple window.

When the patriots in Charlestown saw the two flickering lights, they acted quickly. They sent a rider

This lantern has been identified as one of the lanterns that hung in the steeple of the Old North Church in Boston on the night of April 18, 1775.

to Lexington to warn John Hancock and Samuel Adams. But this rider never got to Lexington. British soldiers may have stopped him.

Paul, meanwhile, went to his home on North Square, not far from the Old North Church. He told his family what he was planning to do. Then Paul put on riding boots and a heavy cape.

He kissed his wife and left. As he went out the door, his dog trailed after him.

As Paul would later recall, "I went to the North part of town where I had kept a boat."

Again, Paul had friends who helped him. He met them near the pier.

At this point, according to legend, Paul suddenly remembered that he had forgotten his spurs. Fortunately, Paul's dog was there. Paul is said to have written a note to his wife and pinned it to the dog's collar. Then he sent the dog trotting home. After several minutes, the dog returned. Paul's spurs were around his neck.

Another piece of folklore recalls that Paul also forgot to bring cloth to wrap around the handles of the oars. This was to muffle the sound of oars as they moved back and forth in the oarlocks.

Again Paul was blessed with good fortune. One of his friends went to the nearby home of a young lady he knew. He called out to her from the street and told her what was needed. Immediately, she pulled off the long woolen underwear she was wearing and tossed it out the window. Paul and his friends ripped the underwear in two and wrapped each piece around an oar.

Once this was done, Paul and two of his friends got into the boat and pushed off into the river. They rowed silently toward a landing just north of Charlestown. Their route enabled them to keep as far away as possible from the British warship *Somerset*.

As they rowed, Paul and his friends could see the dark shape of the *Somerset*. The moon, nearly full, was rising behind them. Paul worried that its light would make them easy to spot. But Paul's tiny boat managed to slip past the huge vessel without being seen.

When they reached the landing near Charlestown,

Paul's friends dropped him off. He walked the short distance into town. There he met members of the Sons of Liberty. They told Paul they had seen the signal lights from the Old North Church.

Paul then went to borrow a horse from Deacon John Larkin, a local patriot. The horse was a fine mare. She was big, strong, and fast. She is thought to have been named Brown Beauty.

Before Paul left, he spoke with Richard Devens,

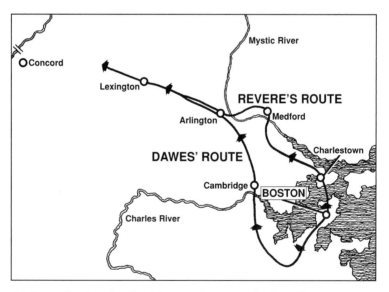

On his midnight ride, Paul Revere first went by boat from Boston to Charlestown, then continued on horseback toward Lexington and Concord. William Dawes took a land route.

one of the patriot leaders in Charlestown. Devens warned Paul of the British officers who were guarding the road to Lexington. Devens described them as "nine officers of the ministerial army, mounted on good horses, and armed. . . ."

"I set off upon a very good horse," Paul was to write. "It was then about 11 o'clock, and very pleasant." Indeed, the night was pleasantly mild, with signs of spring in the air.

Paul kept Brown Beauty at a fast trot as he headed north. He sped across Charlestown Neck. He then turned west.

All was going well when suddenly he saw two men on horseback. They were under a big tree by the side of the road. As he drew closer, he could see that they were British officers.

Paul yanked hard on the reins to stop Brown Beauty. He then raced off in the other direction. But the British officers had spotted Paul.

"One tryed to git a head of Me, and the other to take me," Paul wrote. "I turned my horse very quick, and Galloped towards Charlestown neck, and then pushed for the Medford Road. The one who chased me, endeavoring to Cut me off, got into a Clay pond, near where the new Tavern is now built. I got clear of him. . . ."

The other officer tried to catch Paul. But thanks to Brown Beauty's speed, the officer was soon left behind.

Out of trouble, Paul followed the Mystic Road toward Medford, Menotomy [Arlington], and Lexington. He had traveled the same road two days before and knew it well.

At around midnight, Paul arrived at the home of the Reverend Jonas Clarke in Lexington. John Hancock and Samuel Adams were staying with the Clarke family.

Sergeant William Munroe, a local militiaman, guarded the door. The sergeant did not know Paul Revere. He ordered him to quiet down. The family "had just retired," he declared, and did not want to be disturbed by "any noise about the house."

"Noise!" Paul exclaimed. "You'll have noise enough before long. The regulars [British professional soldiers] are coming out!"

Paul got down from his horse and banged on the front door of the Clarke house. From a downstairs window, the head of the Reverend Clarke appeared. He wanted to know who was there.

From inside the house, John Hancock shouted, "Come in, Revere! We're not afraid of *you*."

Paul entered the house to be greeted by Hancock and Adams. He wasted no time in delivering his words of warning. The British troops were on their way. As the three men talked, William Dawes arrived.

Revere and Dawes remained at Lexington for another hour or so. Then they set out for Concord, several miles to the west.

On the road, the two riders met Samuel Prescott. Prescott was a young Concord doctor. He was also a member of the Sons of Liberty. After learning of their mission, Dr. Prescott offered to join them.

Some books say that Paul's words of warning to the colonists were, "The British are coming!" Not so, according to modern-day historians. After all, the people of the Massachusetts Bay Colony thought of themselves as being British. A call of

One artist's version of Paul Revere's arrival at the Clarke house in Lexington, where John Hancock and Samuel Adams were staying. A local militiaman was guarding the front door.

"The British are coming!" would not have made any sense to them.

"The regulars are coming out! The regulars are coming out!" That's what Paul Revere and his companions shouted to the citizens as they hurried along the road to Concord.

LEXINGTON AND CONCORD

THE THREE MEN RODE ON AT A RAPID pace. For a time all went well. Then trouble in the form of more British officers and soldiers loomed.

Paul tells what happened next:

When we had got about half way from Lexington to Concord, the other two, stopped at a House to awake the man. I kept along. When I had got about 200 yards ahead of them, I saw two officers under a tree as before.

I immediately called to my company to come up, saying here was two of them. In an instant I saw four officers, who rode up to me, with their pistols in their hands & said . . . you stop, if you go an inch further you are a dead Man. . . .

Doctor [Prescott] jumped his horse over a low stone wall, and got to Concord. I observed a wood at a small distance and made for that intending when I gained that to jump my Horse & run afoot, just as I reached it out started six officers, siesed my bridle, put their pistols to my Breast, ordered me to dismount, which I did.

One of them, who appeared to have command there . . . asked where I came from; I told him. He asked me what time I left it; I told him, he seemed much surprised.

He said Sir may I crave your name?

I answered my name is Revere.

What, said he, Paul Revere?

I answered yes . . . he told me not to be afraid, no one should hurt me.

When the officers went after Paul and Dr. Prescott, William Dawes galloped off in the opposite direction. Two British officers went after him.

Dawes spotted a farmhouse. He hurried toward it. When he reached the farmhouse, he stopped so abruptly he was thrown forward and out of the saddle.

As he got to his feet, Dawes shouted "Hel-lo!" He was hoping to get the attention of the people inside the farmhouse.

The British officers thought that Dawes was getting help. They turned their horses and fled.

The dark farmhouse turned out to be empty. Dawes returned to Lexington. Only Dr. Prescott got to Concord.

Paul, meanwhile, was ordered to get back up on his horse. Then Major Edward Mitchel, who was in charge of the British officers, rode up and took the reins out of Paul's hands. He gave them to another officer, who was assigned to lead Paul.

Paul continues: "I asked him to let me have the reins & I would not run from him, he said he would not trust me."

Paul was put in the center of a group of colonists that the soldiers had captured earlier in the evening. Then the group started off toward Lexington.

Not long after he left Lexington for Concord, Paul Revere was captured by British officers.

"We are now going toward your friends," Paul was told, "and if you attempt to run..."

He threatened Paul's life. Paul was calm. "I told him," Paul would recall, "he might do as he pleased."

As they got closer to town, they heard gunfire.

"What was that?" an officer asked.

Paul explained that it was a warning shot. It was meant to serve as a signal that the regulars were drawing near.

Major Mitchel frowned. He did not like the idea of being cut off from the main body of British troops if there was going to be trouble. He decided that he and his men had better flee.

Before leaving, the British forced Paul to give Brown Beauty to them. Then they rode off. A sergeant rode Brown Beauty. They left Paul alone and horseless.

Paul wondered what to do next. He chose not to go to Concord; it was too far away. He decided instead to go back to Lexington and find out what had happened to Sam Adams and John Hancock.

It was around three o'clock in the morning. It was cold, damp, and very dark.

Paul made his way through the countryside, climbing over stone walls and crossing pastures. Outside of Lexington, he passed through the town's burial ground. Dawn was approaching by the time he reached the Clarke home.

Paul found that Adams and Hancock were still there. He begged them to leave right away. They finally climbed into Hancock's carriage. They then headed for the town of Woburn, northwest of Lexington.

Paul went with them. But he traveled only part of the way. When he felt that Adams and Hancock were out of danger, Paul left the carriage and returned to the Clarke house. He wanted to rest and have something to eat. He also wanted to, as he put it, "find out what was acting."

He had not been at the Clarke house very long when a young man named John Lowell appeared. Lowell was John Hancock's clerk. He pleaded with Paul to help him with a vital task.

Lowell explained that when Hancock had fled he had left behind a large trunk filled with important papers. The trunk was at the Buckman Tavern in Lexington, not far from where they were now. It had to be taken from the tavern before British soldiers discovered it.

Would Paul help him move the trunk to a safe place? Paul said he would.

John Hancock's trunk, left behind at the Buckman Tavern. The trunk is now in the hands of the Worcester Historical Museum.

The sun had broken over the horizon. The townspeople of Lexington were making frantic preparations for the arrival of the regulars. A drummer beat out the call to arms. Sixty or seventy Lexington militiamen, highly trained soldiers, were gathering on the Lexington Green. Women and children watched from their doorways.

But all that Paul could think of was the trunk. He and John Lowell hurried to the Buckman Tavern. In a room on the second floor, they found the trunk. It was right where John Hancock had left it.

From an upper window, Paul looked out to see the red-coated British regulars approaching. There were hundreds of them. They marched in a long, orderly column. They were heading for the Lexington Green.

Major John Pitcairn rode at the head of the marching men. Paul knew him well. Pitcairn was a North Square neighbor of his.

Paul watched for only a few moments. He had a job to do. He turned to the trunk. It was very big, about four feet long and two feet wide, with a curved lid. And it was very heavy.

Paul and John Lowell decided to carry the trunk from the tavern and hide it in the woods. They strained every muscle to lift it. Then they struggled to get it down the stairs.

Outside, the militiamen were forming into two long ranks. Paul and John Lowell walked through the battle lines carrying the trunk. The regulars were beginning to draw near. No one seemed to notice them.

Paul passed close to Captain James Parker, who commanded the militiamen. He heard Parker say, "Let the troops pass by and don't molest them without they begin first." In other words, Parker was saying do not fire unless fired upon.

As Paul and John Lowell reached the far end of the green with the trunk, Paul heard a shot ring out behind him. "A gun was fired," Paul would later write. "I heard the report and turned my head." But a building blocked Paul's view. He could not tell who fired first.

Then Paul heard a loud shout and then a volley of shots. Eight militiamen fell dead. Ten others were wounded. A British soldier was also wounded.

Paul did not stop to think of the great importance of the moment. He did not consider that he had witnessed the first shots to be fired in the struggle of the American colonists to win their independence. Paul's job was to get John Hancock's trunk to a safe place. That's what he was thinking about.

After the clash at Lexington, the British regulars marched on to Concord. The militiamen there had

The opening battle of the Revolutionary War at Lexington Green.

been alerted by Dr. Prescott hours before. They were waiting for the British.

Hundreds of militiamen met a group of redcoats at North Bridge not far from Concord. After a brief skirmish in which three British soldiers and two

Americans were killed, the British turned back to Boston.

By now, the entire countryside was ready to join the battle. Men by the hundreds grabbed their muskets and hurried toward Concord. From behind stone walls, fences, trees, and barns, they fired at the British column. Redcoats fell in their tracks. This continued until the redcoats got back to Boston.

Paul had stayed at Lexington only long enough to hear the first shots fired. Then he and John Lowell, in Paul's words, "made off" with Hancock's trunk. The two men must have been successful in getting the trunk stored away safely, although they never spoke or wrote about what happened to it.

The day after the bloodshed at Lexington and Concord, Paul was on hand when Dr. Warren and other colonial leaders met in Cambridge. They discussed what must be done to assure victory in the struggle ahead.

Dr. Warren asked Paul whether he might be willing to do "out of doors business." Paul said he would. Over the next three weeks, Paul traveled throughout New England delivering messages in service of the colonial cause.

Word quickly spread that American colonists and British troops had fired upon one another at Lexington and Concord. Men throughout the colonies began to take up arms. On June 16, 1775, the Continental Congress named George Washington to command the Continental army.

Meanwhile, Dr. Warren had learned that the British under General Gage planned to occupy the hills overlooking Boston. If successful, they would gain control of the city and its harbor.

The Americans moved first. Their plan was to fortify Boston's Bunker Hill. Instead, they dug in on Breed's Hill, which was closer to the city.

On the afternoon of June 17, 1775, British troops led by General William Howe launched an assault against the colonists' position on Breed's Hill. The colonists fought gallantly, driving back two British charges. Then the colonists ran out of gunpowder. With a third attack, the British forced the colonists to flee.

What came to be called the Battle of Bunker Hill in June 1775 was the bloodiest battle of the Revolutionary War.

More than 1,000 British troops and about 400 colonists were killed or wounded during the fighting. It was the bloodiest battle of the Revolutionary War.

In history books, the battle is wrongly named. It is called the Battle of Bunker Hill. It should be known as the Battle of Breed's Hill.

In the battle's final stages, the Americans lost a brave leader. Dr. Joseph Warren, who had insisted on joining the fight, was shot and killed. Dr. Warren had written and spoken on behalf of the patriot cause for more than a decade.

Dr. Warren's death deeply saddened Paul. Among the colonial leaders, no one was closer to Paul. Two years after his passing, Paul honored him by naming his newborn son Joseph Warren Revere.

CHAPTER 8

WAR YEARS

THE AMERICAN REVOLUTION BEGAN on the morning of April 19, 1775. That's when the colonists and British regulars opened fire on one another at Lexington Green.

The war lasted more than eight years. It did not end until September 3, 1783. On that date, the British signed the Treaty of Paris. In so doing, they accepted the United States as an independent nation.

During the war, Paul Revere kept very busy. He seldom worked as a silversmith, however. There was little need for fine silver bowls or teapots.

Instead, he continued to serve as a rider. He helped the colonists as an engraver. And he made gunpowder. Paul also played a military role. He was a colonel in the Massachusetts militia.

Paul Revere remained best known, however, for his midnight ride. The ride would sweep him into the pages of history.

In the early stages of the war, Boston was under British military rule. As a result, the patriot leaders moved the capital of Massachusetts out of Boston. Watertown became the new capital. About eight miles to the west, Watertown was a small farming town. The Provincial Congress began holding its meetings in Watertown. Many patriot leaders moved there.

George Washington took command of the Continental army at Cambridge, Massachusetts, on July 3, 1775. One of his first goals was to drive the British out of Boston.

The Reveres moved into the John Cook house in Watertown in May 1775. The family now included Paul, his wife, Rachel, and their six children. Paul's mother also lived with them.

Paul's fifteen-year-old son stayed in Boston. His job was to look after the house on North Square.

The war caused many problems for Massachusetts. In mid-1775, the colony found itself in need of paper money. The money would be used to pay soldiers and other bills.

The colony turned to Paul. He was asked to make the copperplates from which the paper money would be printed.

Paul set up a workplace in the Cook house where he and his family lived. There he made the copperplates and printed the money.

Young John Cook helped Paul. Guests who were staying with the Cooks sometimes helped, too.

Paul had to work in secrecy. If the British were to find out that he was printing money for the colony, they would be sure to deal roughly with him.

Paul had problems. The printing plates were made of copper and copper was very scarce.

It was the same with paper. Sometimes there was not enough paper. What could be bought was very expensive.

The colony once refused to pay for the costly paper. Paul had to pay with his own money.

As he wrote, "The paper for the last, cost me Six dollars a Rheam [ream] when I did not expect to give but four... the Committee of the House ordered the paper to be made & did not agree for the price. & I was obliged to pay the paper maker his demand."

Paper money wasn't all that the colonists needed. They also faced a shortage of gunpowder. At Breed's Hill, the lack of gunpowder was very costly. If the colonists had not run out of gunpowder, they might have won the battle.

During the French and Indian War, gunpowder was not a problem. Colonial riflemen had gotten their gunpowder from the British. Now the colonists were going to have to get their powder somewhere else.

Much gunpowder was made in and near Philadelphia. In November 1775, the colony of

Massachusetts sent Paul Revere to Philadelphia. There he was to meet with a man who owned a powder-making factory. The man's name was Oswald Eve. It was hoped that he would tell Paul what he needed to know to build a mill for making gunpowder in Massachusetts.

Once Paul arrived in Philadelphia, he met with Oswald Eve. The meeting did not go well. Oswald Eve did not wish to share what he knew with Paul. Eve was making good money selling gunpowder to the colonists. He did not want Paul Revere or anyone else trying to do the same thing.

Eve, however, did give Paul a quick tour of his powder mill. But he would not allow Paul to study the machinery. And he would not let Paul talk to any of the workers.

Yet Paul was still able to learn a great deal. Sam Adams helped, too. He got plans for a gunpowder mill for Paul. Paul was then able to design a powder mill for Massachusetts.

The mill was built in Canton, about fifteen miles south of Boston. By May 1776, the plant was making

powder. It was soon making most of the powder used
by Massachusetts's troops.

During the time Paul was working on the powder
plant, the Continental army was on the move. In
May 1775, the colonists scored an important victory
over the British at Fort Ticonderoga in New York
State. After the battle, the patriots captured many
cannons.

*Colonel Henry Knox's men hauling to Boston artillery captured at Fort
Ticonderoga.*

Afterward, Colonel Henry Knox set forth a bold plan. He wanted to haul the captured cannons by sled over the snow-covered Berkshire Mountains of Massachusetts. The weapons would then be taken east across the state to Boston. General Washington approved the plan.

During the winter, the colonists put the plan into action. Teams of oxen began pulling huge sleds carrying the cannons over the mountains. By late January 1776, the weapons had gotten as far as Framingham, Massachusetts. Boston was only twenty or so miles away.

The colonists didn't stop at Framingham. They tugged the heavy guns up the hills just south of Boston. The work was done in secret at night. By March 4, 1776, the guns were in place.

General William Howe was in charge of the British troops in Boston. When he learned those huge cannons were pointing down at him and his troops, he groaned. He knew that the British could no longer defend the city.

General Howe ordered the British "to quit the

town." On Sunday morning, March 17, 1776, General Howe began loading his troops onto ships. Before the day had ended, they had left Boston forever.

With the British gone, Paul and his family were able to move back to their home on North Square.

Two favorite SONGS,

made on the Evacuation of the Town of BOSTON,

by the *Britiſh Troops*, on the 17th of March, 1776.

IN ſeventeen hundred and ſeventy ſix,
  On March the eleventh, the time was prefix'd,
Our forces march'd on upon Dorcheſter-neck,
Made fortifications againſt an attack.
  The morning next following, as Howe did eſpy,
The banks we caſt up, were ſo copious and high,
Said he in three months, all my men with their might,
Cou'd not make two ſuch Forts as they've made in a night.
  Now we hear that their Admiral was very wroth,
And drawing his ſword, he bids Howe to go forth,
And drive off the YANKEES from Dorcheſter hill:
Or he'd leave the harbour and him to their will.
  Howe rallies his forces upon the next day,

IT was'nt our will that Bunker Hill
  From us ſhould e,er be taken:
We thought 'twould never be retook,
  But w. find we are Miſtaken.

The ſoldiers bid the hill farewell,
  Two images left ſentreis,
This they had done all out of fun
  To the American Yankees.

A flag of truce was ſent thereon,
  To ſee if the hill was clear,
No living ſoul was found thereon,
  But theſe images ſtood there.

A handbill issued to celebrate the departure of the British from Boston.

Although the British had been in Boston for only eleven months, they had caused great changes. Everywhere British soldiers had dug trenches and built earthen shelters. These were to be used in case the Americans attacked.

The British troops had cut down most of Boston's trees. They used the wood for fires for heating and cooking. More than a few wooden houses had been torn down for firewood.

The British had looted many homes. Furniture and anything else made of wood had been chopped up for fuel. Valuables were gone.

But Paul's house had not been looted. Looked after by his son, it had escaped without damage.

INTO BATTLE

Once Paul Revere returned to Boston with his family, his life changed. On April 8, 1776, not long after the British troops had left the city, he became an officer in the Massachusetts militia. He held the rank of major. He served as a militia officer for several years.

Paul was happy to be a member of the state militia. He was proud when he was promoted to the rank of lieutenant colonel. But what Paul Revere really wanted to be was an officer with the Continental army. He wanted a chance to serve with General Washington.

Paul Revere seemed to have the skills needed to make a good army officer. He had the know-how, having served in the French and Indian War. He could point to long service as a faithful patriot. He had the respect of the patriot leaders.

He was bright. He was a hard worker. He was in good physical condition.

Paul asked his friends to help him. They did not.

In 1777, in a letter to John Lamb, a longtime friend, Paul wrote, "I did expect before this to have been in the Continental Army, but do assure you, I have never been taken notice of, by those whom I thought my friends, [and] am obliged to be contented in this States service."

For most of his time with the state militia, Paul Revere was in charge of an island fort. It guarded the entrance to Boston Harbor. The fort was named the Castle.

It was not an exciting job. The British were no longer interested in Boston. New York had become the center of attention. General Washington believed that the British would make "no attempt on Massachusetts Bay."

The Castle was all but forgotten. Hardly anyone

On July 4, 1776, the Continental Congress adopted the Declaration of Independence, and the United States was born. In this scene, the Declaration is being read to Washington's army in New York on July 9, 1776.

paid any attention to Paul and the men he commanded. They were working to prepare themselves for a battle that was never going to take place.

Paul's men got bored. Some soldiers simply

walked away from the Castle and never returned. These men were called deserters.

On September 27, 1777, Paul and the men he commanded were called into action. They received orders to march to Newport, Rhode Island. They were given the task of chasing British troops out of Newport. By so doing, they would be preventing a possible attack on Boston.

Paul and his men marched to Newport, a distance of about seventy miles. But they never saw any British troops. They returned home without firing a shot.

Paul and his regiment were sent to Rhode Island a second time in August 1778. While he was away, Paul wrote to Rachel. In the letter, Paul described how pained he felt being separated from his wife, "whom I so tenderly love, and from my little lambs."

But Paul felt it was his duty to serve. "Were I at home," he said in the letter, "I should want to be here."

His letter continued: "I hope the affair will soon be settled; I think it will not be long first. I trust the

Allwise Being who has protected me will still protect me, and send me safely to the Arms of her whom it is my greatest happiness to call my own."

In the summer of 1779, Paul got a chance to prove his value as a battlefield commander. Plans were announced to remove British troops from Fort George on the Castine Peninsula in Penobscot Bay in Maine. (At the time, Maine was a part of Massachusetts.) Fort George put in danger ships that were heading to and from Massachusetts.

A huge fleet was brought together to support the operation. It included nineteen armed ships and twenty-one transports. The ships had 344 guns. The transports carried more than 1,000 soldiers. It was America's biggest seagoing operation of the entire war. Paul was aboard a vessel named the *Spring Bird*.

The American fleet arrived at Penobscot Bay on July 25, 1779. Three days later, several hundred American soldiers were put ashore. Their orders were to attack and capture Fort George. Paul and his men were part of the attacking force.

British cannons within the fort killed and

wounded many Americans. Still, the Americans managed to climb a cliff and get their guns in place for a final attack.

But the attack never got started. Before it began, the army commanders asked the navy's warships to start firing at three British warships sitting in the Penobscot River. The commander of the American fleet refused. He didn't want his ships to attract British fire. The army was afraid to attack with the British ships so near.

Day after day, the disagreement between the American land and naval forces continued. Meanwhile, the British were working to make their fort stronger.

Paul was losing hope. He was in favor of ending the operation. As he would write, "It always was my sentiment, that if we could not Dislodge the Enemy in seven days, we ought to Quit the ground. For Where the Enemy has the command of the Sea, we ought not to have risqued [risked] so much as we did."

American ground and naval forces still could not

agree. Suddenly, seven British warships sailed into view. They fired on the American fleet.

The American ships tried to escape. But they could not. Some American ships were set on fire and sank. Others crashed into the rocky beaches. The entire fleet was lost. Paul Revere escaped on the *Spring Bird*. When the ship could go no further, he came ashore near the town of Frankfort.

On the ground, over 500 Americans lost their

The American fleet, here seeking to flee British warships, suffered a crushing defeat during the Penobscot Bay expedition. Fourteen vessels were burned or beached; more than twenty were captured.

lives or were wounded or taken prisoner. Footsore and weary, the rest returned to Boston months later.

What happened to the Americans at Penobscot Bay was not Paul Revere's fault. But almost everyone who had anything to do with the disaster was made to share the blame, including Paul.

In the months that followed his return to Boston, Paul was dismissed from the Massachusetts militia. He was also called upon to defend his actions. He was told he had not followed orders. He was even told that he had acted in a cowardly manner.

Paul fought the attacks. Time after time, he asked to be tried by a military court. He wanted a ruling to be made on the charges against him.

Paul's request was finally granted in 1782. Following the trial, he was cleared of any wrongdoing.

The trial helped Paul Revere restore his reputation. But he was never able to look back upon his military career and call it a success.

NEW VENTURES

TODAY, PAUL REVERE IS BEST KNOWN for his midnight ride. He is also praised for his work as a silversmith. Yet Paul Revere also did many important things after the Revolutionary War.

Paul was forty-eight years old when the Revolutionary War ended. He found that his work as a silversmith no longer satisfied him as it once did. He needed something more.

Paul began handing over more and more of his work to his oldest son, Paul Revere III, and to others who worked in the shop. In 1783, Paul III became his father's partner.

Paul Revere tried other businesses. He began selling hardware. From England, he bought birdcages, playing cards, writing paper, brass candlesticks, and other items. He then sold these in his hardware shop.

Paul tried other businesses. In November 1788, he opened a foundry in the shipyard district of North Boston. He was soon making nails, hammers, bolts, and spikes out of molten metal.

Paul wrote, "We have got our furna[ce] agoing, and have no doubt the business will do exceedingly well in Boston."

Paul kept active in politics. Indeed, he was looked upon as the political leader of Boston's craftsmen. These men called themselves "mechanics."

The mechanics of Boston were strong Federalists. They supported the Federal Constitution. The Constitution was the new plan of government that had been drawn up in Philadelphia.

Congress sent the document to the states for approval. Nine of the thirteen states were needed to ratify—or approve—the Constitution in order for it to become law.

Early in 1788, the Constitution came up for

A trade card given out by Paul Revere advertised his foundry's many different products.

approval in Massachusetts. Boston's mechanics were afraid that Sam Adams would vote against the Constitution.

The mechanics held a mass meeting at the Green Dragon, a large, brick Boston tavern. When they voted, every man agreed that the Constitution should be adopted.

After the meeting, the mechanics marched through the streets of Boston to Sam Adams's house. They wanted to tell him how they had voted.

Adams was cautious. "How many," he asked, "were gathered together when this resolution was [passed]?"

"More, sir, than the Green Dragon could hold," Paul answered.

"And where were the rest, Mr. Revere?"

"In the streets, sir."

"And how many in the streets?"

"More, sir, than there are stars in the sky."

Sam Adams decided to vote in favor of the Constitution. In February 1788, Massachusetts became the sixth state to ratify the Constitution. The vote was close, 187 to 168.

To celebrate, the mechanics held a parade. Paul and other leaders of the Boston mechanics rode in a handsome sleigh that was drawn by four horses. Behind the sleigh marched blacksmiths, carpenters, barrel makers, shipwrights, and other craftsmen.

While Paul often worked for the public good, he was always seeking new ways of doing business. In 1792, Paul began using his foundry to make church bells. At the time, Paul was a member of the Second

Church of Boston. The church had no bell of its own. Its bell came from the Old North Meeting House. The British had destroyed the meeting house during the war.

The bell was very big. It weighed 500 pounds. But the bell had a crack in it. No one was permitted to ring the bell except in case of fire.

The members of Paul's church asked him to melt down the bell and remold it.

Thirty-five members of the church promised to donate enough money to pay for the work. Jokingly, the members voted that anyone who failed to make his promised donation would have to pay a penalty. He would not be allowed to hear the bell.

Making a bell is something like making a cake. A bell-maker has to know the right ingredients, how long to keep it in the furnace, and how long to cool the hot metal.

Paul read books and articles to learn about bell making. He talked with bell-making experts.

Even so, Paul's first bell did not turn out too well. It had a shrill, high-pitched sound.

This 900-pound bell, from 1804, is one of twenty-three bells known to exist that were cast during the time that Paul Revere was personally involved with the foundry. It can be seen in the courtyard of the Revere House in Boston.

Some of the members of Paul's church said that it wasn't a great bell for church services. It was better for calling people out for fires.

Yet Paul was proud of his bell. On it, he put, "The first church bell cast in Boston 1792 by P. Revere." In time, Boston became proud of the bell, too.

Between 1792 and 1828, the Revere foundry cast more than 950 bells. One of these, produced in 1816, hangs in the steeple of Boston's King's Chapel. It still rings each Sunday. To Paul, it was "the sweetest bell we ever made."

Paul wrote many notes and letters about his bells. He was proud of their high quality. In one of his letters, he declared, "We know we can cast as good bells as can be cast in the world, both for goodness & for sound."

Paul's success as a silversmith and with the foundry enabled him to enjoy a comfortable life. In 1799, Paul bought a handsome three-story brick house for the family on Charter Street in Boston. Not long after, he sold the old house on North Square.

Paul and Rachel were not alone in their new home. Five of their children, three of whom were teenagers, moved in with them. So did three of their grandchildren.

Joshua, at twenty-six, was the oldest of the Revere children to live at home with his mother and father. Joseph Warren was three years younger. John, the youngest, was thirteen. Harriet was seventeen, and Maria was fifteen.

As the new century dawned, Paul, at sixty-five, started another new business. He planned to develop a mill for producing sheet copper. Sheet copper was important. It was used to protect the outside of ships and the roofs of large buildings from rotting.

Paul Revere appears comfortable and prosperous in this portrait, painted by French artist Charles-Balthazar-Julien-Févret de Saint-Mémin in Philadelphia around 1800.

Others had tried such a venture. None had succeeded.

Although he was quite well-to-do at the time, the new business put a strain on Paul's finances. As he wrote, "I have engaged to build me a Mill for Rolling Copper into sheets which for me is a great undertaking, and will require every farthing which I can rake or scrape."

The copper mill was erected in Canton,

Paul Revere's rolling mill provided the copper sheeting for the dome of the Massachusetts State House in Boston. The dome was later covered with gold leaf.

Massachusetts, on the property where Paul's old powder mill once stood. Paul put $25,000 of his own money into the business. But that wasn't enough. He also had to borrow $10,000 from the federal government. By 1801, the copper mill was in full operation.

Much of Paul Revere's rolled copper went to shipbuilders. In 1803, the hull of the *Constitution*, the flagship of the American fleet, needed new copper. The navy went to Paul for the *Constitution*'s copper.

The Revere Copper Company also furnished heavy sheets of copper to Robert Fulton for boilers for his steamboats. It was Fulton who built the *Clermont*, launched in 1807. The *Clermont* was the first successful steamboat to operate in American waters.

In the space of hardly more than ten years, Paul Revere had managed to start up and operate one of the first industries of its type in America. He had once said that if he could obtain the copper he needed and the money to buy his furnaces, he could "make [himself] a master of this business." Paul Revere had done just that.

AT CANTON DALE

I N THEIR LATER YEARS, PAUL REVERE and his wife retired to Canton, where his copper mill was located. There he and Rachel lived in a plain, two-story wood-frame house. They called their home "Canton Dale."

At Canton Dale, Paul's time was given over to his family and friends. Around 1810, Paul wrote a poem describing the simple pleasures of life there. It begins:

Not distant far from Taunton road
In Canton Dale is my abode.
My Cot [house] 'tho small, my mind's at ease,
My Better Half, takes pains to please,
Content sits lolling in her chair,

This pen-and-ink drawing, possibly sketched by Paul Revere, depicts his copper mill and home in Canton, Massachusetts.

And all my friends find welcome there
When they git home they never fail,
To praise the charms of Canton Dale.

On June 18, 1812, Paul's peaceful life began to change. The United States went to war against Great Britain. It was called the War of 1812. Some called it "the second war of independence."

During the summer of 1814, the city of Washington was captured and burned by the British. The people of Boston became fearful. They felt they also might be attacked.

Paul Revere offered to help in the war effort. He was one of the first of 150 mechanics to offer to work without pay to strengthen the defenses of Boston. He was almost eighty years old at the time.

Governor Caleb Strong accepted the mechanics' offer. They built Fort Strong on Noddles Island in Boston Harbor.

The War of 1812 ended on December 24, 1814. Fort Strong never had to be put to use in Boston's defense.

Paul Revere served the people of Boston in many other ways. When Boston was struck with an outburst of yellow fever, an often-deadly disease, Paul was named the city's health officer.

Paul's life in retirement was saddened when his son, Paul III, died on January 16, 1813. Five months later, his wife, Rachel, died. She was laid to rest in the Old Granary Burying Ground. Forty years before, Paul had buried his first wife, Sara, there.

This must have been a time for Paul to look back on his long life. He was one of a small handful of the original patriots still alive. The Old Granary Burying

In 1813, Paul Revere's son, Joseph Warren, paid artist Gilbert Stuart $200 to paint these portraits of his parents. Rachel Revere died on June 26 of that year.

Ground also held the graves of John Hancock and Sam Adams.

In 1816, Paul wrote out his will. It began: "In the name of God, Amen. I, Paul Revere, of Boston in the County of Suffolk and Commonwealth of Massachusetts, Esquire, being in good health and of sound memory, but knowing that all men must die do make and declare this to be my last will and testament."

Five of Paul's children were living. He divided most of what he owned equally among them. Small amounts of money went to his grandchildren.

Paul Revere died on May 10, 1818. He was eighty-three years old. He was buried at the Old Granary Burying Ground.

Paul's death took place on a Sunday. Bells of the Boston churches would have been ringing. Hundreds of them had been cast by Paul himself.

Upon his death, the *Boston Intelligencer* called Paul "one of the earliest and most indefatigable Patriots and Soldiers of the Revolution.

"Cool in thought, ardent in action," said the paper, "he was well adapted to form plans, and to carry them into execution—both for the benefit of himself & the service of others."

At the time of his passing, Paul Revere was known in New England as a loyal patriot. He was known for his midnight ride. Bells that he had cast were hanging in the steeples of many New England churches. Pieces of silverware he had crafted were prized in many New England homes.

But Paul Revere was not then a widely known figure. Before the end of the century, however, his importance began to grow. Paul Revere would be on the path toward becoming a legendary American hero.

PAUL REVERE
REMEMBERED

TODAY, THE NAME PAUL REVERE IS A household word. You can sweeten your morning cereal with Revere Sugar. You can order pizza from a Paul Revere Pizza Restaurant (there's "Free Delivery").

You can fry an egg or boil water in one of the many different kinds of cookware known as "Revere Ware." A picture of Paul Revere is stamped on the bottom of each piece.

Paul Revere's name wasn't always so well known. In 1818, the year that he died, Paul Revere was not a national hero. His midnight ride was not considered an important event in American history.

Erected in the city of Boston in 1940, Cyrus Dallin's bronze statue presents Paul Revere as a heroic figure.

"Paul Revere's Ride," a poem by Henry Wadsworth Longfellow, helped to change things. The poem was first published in *The Atlantic Monthly* in January 1861.

At the time, no American poet was more famous than Longfellow was. He had a clear, graceful style. He was a gifted storyteller. He wrote for the average American.

Longfellow's story of Paul Revere as a heroic midnight rider was an instant success. American schoolchildren were required to memorize the poem. Many older Americans can still recite its verses.

Thanks to Longfellow's poem, Paul Revere began to be seen as an American hero.

In 1871, the Boston town of North Chelsea changed its name to Revere. Towns were also named after Paul Revere in Pennsylvania, Minnesota, and Missouri.

In 1875, the United States marked the one-hundredth anniversary of the American Revolution. Many celebrations were held. In honor of the day, President Ulysses S. Grant visited Lexington and

Listen my children, and you shall hear
Of the midnight ride of Paul Revere,
On the eighteenth of April, in Seventy-five;
Hardly a man is now alive
Who remembers that famous day and year.

He said to his friend, "If the British march
By land or sea from the town to-night,
Hang a lantern aloft in the belfry arch
Of the North Church tower as a signal light,—
One if by land, and two if by sea;
And I on the opposite shore will be,
Ready to ride and spread the alarm
Through every Middlesex village and farm,
For the country folk to be up and to arm."
. . . .
So through the night rode Paul Revere;
And so through the night went his cry of alarm
To every Middlesex village and farm,—
A cry of defiance, and not of fear,
A voice in the darkness, a knock at the door,
And a word that shall echo for evermore!
For, borne on the night-wind of the Past,
Through all our history, to the last,
In the hour of darkness and peril and need,
The people will waken and listen to hear
The hurrying hoof-beats of that steed,
And the midnight message of Paul Revere.

Excerpts from "Paul Revere's Ride"
by Henry Wadsworth Longfellow

Longfellow's poem, "Paul Revere's Ride," first published in 1861, helped to make Paul Revere a legendary hero.

Concord. The spotlight again fell on Paul Revere and his famous ride.

During the early 1900s, the Daughters of the American Revolution, a patriotic organization, became interested in Paul Revere. The DAR learned that Paul Revere's home on North Square in Boston was in a broken-down condition. The organization decided to try to rescue the house.

The Paul Revere Memorial Association was founded to rebuild the home, which opened to the public in 1908. It is the only building from the 1600s that remains in what was once "old Boston."

A handsome statue of Paul Revere on his galloping horse stands in Paul Revere Mall in Boston's North End. A long section of the road that Paul Revere traveled on his midnight ride is now a national park.

The anniversary of the midnight ride and the Battle of Lexington is a holiday in Massachusetts and Maine. It's called Patriots' Day. Schools are closed. There are parades, fireworks, and speeches. Special events are scheduled at the Revere House.

Paul Revere's house on North Square in Boston attracts more than 200,000 visitors each year.

Paul Revere's ride is reenacted. The lantern lighting ceremony in the Old North Church is recreated.

And in many Massachusetts cities and towns, church bells are rung that day. Paul Revere would have liked that.

CHRONOLOGY

1734   Paul Revere is born

1754   Paul Revere takes over his father's silversmithing business

1756   Paul Revere serves in the French and Indian War

1757   Paul Revere marries Sara Orne

1764   Sugar Act passed

1765   Stamp Act and Quartering Act passed
       Paul Revere joins the Sons of Liberty

1770   Boston Massacre

1773   Sara Orne Revere dies
       Paul Revere marries Rachel Walker
       Boston Tea Party

1775   Paul Revere's midnight ride
       Battle of Lexington and Concord

1776   Continental Congress adopts the Declaration of Independence

1779   Penobscot expedition fails

1783   Treaty of Paris ends the Revolutionary War

1788   Massachusetts ratifies the Constitution

1792   Paul Revere's foundry starts manufacturing bells

1801   Paul Revere's copper mill begins operating

1813   Rachel Walker Revere dies

1818   Paul Revere dies

1861   Henry Wadsworth Longfellow's poem "Paul Revere's Ride" is published.

1908   Paul Revere's house on North Square is open to the public.

BIBLIOGRAPHY

Fischer, David Hackett. *Paul Revere's Ride*. New York: Oxford University Press, 1994.

Forbes, Esther. *Paul Revere and the World He Lived In*. Boston: Houghton Mifflin, 1942.

Goss, Elbridge Henry. *The Life of Colonel Paul Revere*. 2 vols. Boston: Joseph George Cupples, 1891.

Paul Revere—Artisan, Businessman, and Patriot: The Man Behind the Myth. Boston: Paul Revere Memorial Association, 1988.

Paul Revere's Three Accounts of His Famous Ride. Boston: Massachusetts Historical Society, 1976.

Triber, Jayne E. *A True Republican: The Life of Paul Revere*. Boston: The University of Massachusetts, 1998.

FURTHER READING

Brandt, Keith. *Paul Revere, Son of Liberty*. Mahwah, NJ: Troll Communications, 1990.

Brigham, Clarence S. *Paul Revere's Engravings*. New York: Atheneum, 1969.

Forbes, Esther. *America's Paul Revere*. Boston, MA: Houghton Mifflin, 1946. (Reissue edition, 1990.)

Ford, Barbara. *Paul Revere: Rider for the Revolution*. Springfield, NJ: Enslow Publishers, Inc., 1997.

Fritz, Jean. *And Then What Happened, Paul Revere?* New York: Coward-McCann, 1973.

Lawson, Robert. *Mr. Revere and I*. Boston, MA: Little, Brown and Company, 1988.

Sakurai, Gail. *Paul Revere*. Danbury, CT: Children's Press, 1998.

Stevenson, Augusta. *Paul Revere: Boston Patriot*. New York: Aladdin Paperbacks, 1986.

FOR MORE INFORMATION

American Antiquarian Society
Worcester, Massachusetts
Original copies of more than two dozen of Paul Revere's drawings are owned by the American Antiquarian Society. Write to the society for a list (185 Salisbury Street, Worcester, MA 01609-1634). You can also order photocopies of them.

Massachusetts Historical Society
Boston, Massachusetts
You can get a copy of Paul Revere's description of the ride. It, along with two earlier descriptions, is to be found in a picture book titled *Paul Revere's Three Accounts of His Famous Ride*. For a copy, write to the Massachusetts Historical Society (1154 Boylston Street, Boston, MA 02215).

Paul Revere House
Boston, Massachusetts
The Paul Revere House welcomes almost a quarter of a million visitors each year. Its Web site (http://www.paulreverehouse.org) is growing by leaps and bounds.

Paul Revere Memorial Association
Boston, Massachusetts
For more information about Paul Revere or to become a member of the "Friends of Paul Revere," write to the Paul Revere Memorial Association (19 North Square, Boston, MA 02113).

PHOTO CREDITS

Library of Congress: 6, 21, 28, 42, 74, 109; Bostonian Society: p. 12; Museum of Fine Arts Boston: 16, 25, 30, 36, 45, 115 (left), 115 (right); Old North Church: 18; George Sullivan: 26, 34, 61, 83, 110, 119, 123; Boston Public Library: 40; R.M. Smythe & Co.: 50, 55, 70, 86, 90, 92, 96; Concord Museum: 63; Worcester Historical Society: 77; New York Public Library: 80; National Maritime Museum: 100; Paul Revere Memorial Association: 104, 107; Massachusetts Historical Society: 113.

INDEX

Bold numbers refer to photographs